D1460012

KINGS AND QUEENS

Clare Oliver

p

CONTENTS

This is a Parragon Publishing Book
First published in 2002

Parragon Publishing
Queen Street House
4 Queen Street
Bath BA1 1HE, UK

Copyright © Parragon 2002

Produced by

David West ☆☆ Children's Books
7 Princeton Court
55 Felsham Road
Putney
London SW15 1AZ, UK

All rights reserved. No part of this publication may
be reproduced, stored in a retrieval system, or
transmitted by any means, electronic, mechanical,
photocopying, recording or otherwise, without the
prior permission of the copyright holder.

British Library Cataloguing-in-Publication Data

A catalogue record for this book is available from
the British Library.

ISBN 0-75257-827-8

Printed in Dubai

Designers
Julie Joubinaux, Rob Shone

Illustrators
Neil Reed, Michael Thomas (Allied Artists)

Cartoonist
Peter Wilks (SGA)

Editor
James Pickering

RULE BRITANNIA!

4

WARRIOR KINGS

6

THE NORMAN CONQUEST

8

THE GOOD AND THE BAD

10

FIGHT FOR THE CROWN

12

WHAT A HUSBAND

14

ELIZABETHAN

ENGLAND

16

SCOTTISH KINGS

18

JAMES STUART

20

CIVIL WAR

22

GEORGIAN BRITAIN

24

QUEEN VICTORIA

26

WORLD-WAR KINGS

28

TODAY'S QUEEN

30

INDEX

32

RULE BRITANNIA!

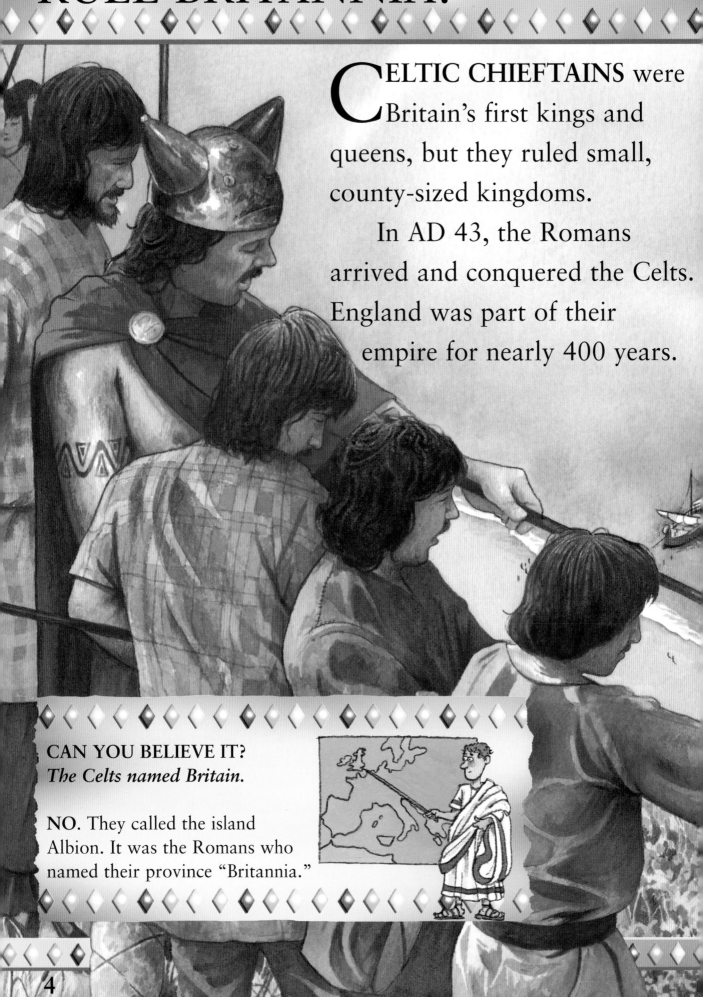

CELTIC CHIEFTAINS were Britain's first kings and queens, but they ruled small, county-sized kingdoms.

In AD 43, the Romans arrived and conquered the Celts. England was part of their empire for nearly 400 years.

CAN YOU BELIEVE IT?
The Celts named Britain.

NO. They called the island Albion. It was the Romans who named their province "Britannia."

As their empire crumbled, Roman soldiers left Britain. New invaders arrived from northern Germany – the Angles, Saxons and Jutes.

Roman galleys
In AD 43 the Roman army landed at Richborough in Kent. Waiting warriors from the most powerful Celtic tribe, the Belgae, were no match for the well-equipped Romans.

KING OF LEGEND

Little is known about the Dark Ages (the centuries just after the Romans left). There are tales about a king called Arthur who fought bravely against the barbarian invaders. In stories, Arthur becomes king because only he can wield the enchanted sword, Excalibur.

YOU MUST BE JOKING!

Celtic kings were buried with their swords – but the weapons were snapped in two. It was a symbol to show a dead king's reign had ended.

WARRIOR KINGS

THE ANGLO-SAXONS slowly forced the Celts into Scotland and Wales. They split England into seven kingdoms.

The Anglo-Saxon kings fought each other until, by AD 829, Egbert of Wessex controlled all of England. But there was still no peace – now there were Danish Vikings to face instead! The ruler who fought them best was Egbert's grandson, Alfred.

Alfred the Great Alfred ruled England from 871 until 900. He managed to defeat the Vikings and find peace – for a time. One legend tells how Alfred went into the Danish camp disguised as a harp-player, to overhear the Danes' battle plans.

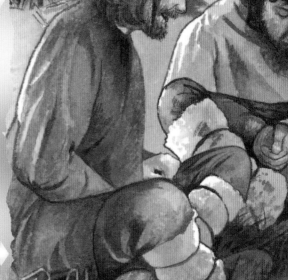

CAN YOU BELIEVE IT?
Offa's Dyke was built to keep out water.

NO. It was a wall of earth built in the 780s to keep the Welsh out of Mercia, one of the seven Anglo-Saxon kingdoms.

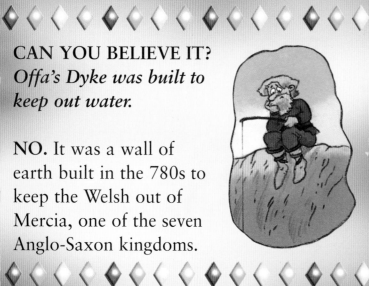

VIKING PILLAGERS

The Vikings were warriors from Norway, Denmark and Sweden. They raided England throughout the 800s and 900s, seizing land and looting treasure. In 1016, the Danish king Canute took over the English throne and made England part of his Scandinavian empire.

YOU MUST BE JOKING!
King Canute tried to turn back the waves! He wanted to show his slimy courtiers that God was more powerful than he was.

THE NORMAN CONQUEST

EARLY IN 1066 Edward the Confessor died and a new king was crowned – Harold II. But William, the Duke of Normandy, had also been promised the throne and he came across from France to claim it.

During his rule, William did the first proper survey of England. His men rode about the land, measuring fields and counting people and animals. All their findings were written in the Domesday Book of 1086.

Building the tower
The Normans built hundreds of castles, including the Tower of London. They built cathedrals, too, and a church for every parish. Many Norman buildings still stand.

THE BATTLE OF HASTINGS

William landed at Pevensey, Sussex, on September 28 1066. A fortnight later he met Harold and his men at Battle, near Hastings. The French won the day. William marched straight to London and was crowned there on Christmas Day – King of England at last!

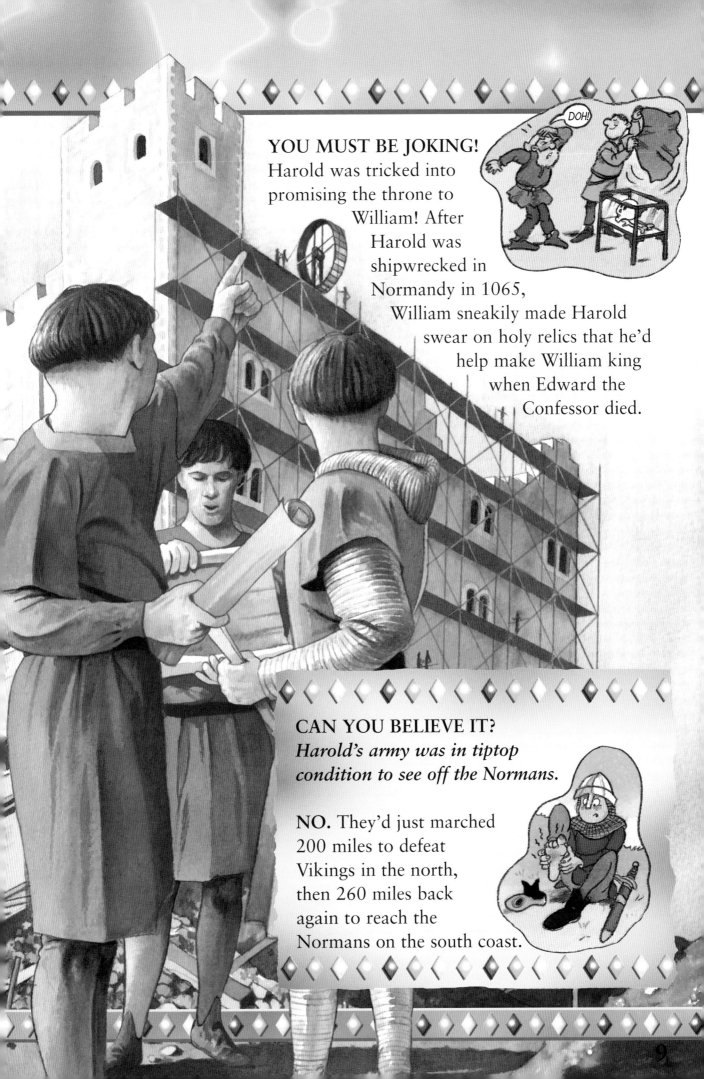

YOU MUST BE JOKING!
Harold was tricked into promising the throne to William! After Harold was shipwrecked in Normandy in 1065, William sneakily made Harold swear on holy relics that he'd help make William king when Edward the Confessor died.

DOH!

CAN YOU BELIEVE IT?
Harold's army was in tiptop condition to see off the Normans.

NO. They'd just marched 200 miles to defeat Vikings in the north, then 260 miles back again to reach the Normans on the south coast.

9

THE GOOD AND THE BAD

RICHARD I AND JOHN were brothers who ruled about 800 years ago. Richard was admired for his bravery – but he wasn't so good for his people. He neglected them to go off on Crusades (holy wars).

When Richard died, John became king. He was unpopular for demanding high taxes, but he wasn't really a bad ruler. It was just that his brother Richard had spent everything in his endless wars.

The Magna Carta
In 1215 the English barons were fed up with paying high taxes to John and having to supply men for his army. They made John agree to a long list of demands, which became the Magna Carta (Great Charter).

YOU MUST BE JOKING!

Richard was captured on his way home from the Holy Wars and English peasants had to cough up to free him! A quarter of everyone's income went toward Richard's ransom.

ROBIN HOOD

No one knows whether Robin Hood really existed, but he's said to have lived during Richard I's reign. According to legend, Robin lived with his band of followers in Sherwood Forest, Nottingham. He was an outlaw, who stole from the rich and gave to the poor.

CAN YOU BELIEVE IT?
During his ten-year reign, Richard I was only in England for a few months!

YES. He was too busy fighting the Crusades against the Sultan Saladin.

FIGHT FOR THE CROWN

Battle of Bosworth
On August 22 1485 a fierce battle was fought near the town of Bosworth in Leicestershire. With just 8,000 men, Henry Tudor defeated King Richard III's 12,000-strong army.

THE WARS OF THE ROSES (1455–1485) were a struggle between two branches of the royal family, York and Lancaster. Their emblems were white and red roses. Each side believed it should rule England.

CAN YOU BELIEVE IT?
You've played "Snap!" with Henry VII's wife!

YES. Elizabeth of York was the model for the drawing of the Queen on our packs of cards!

When Henry Tudor became king Henry VII, the struggle finally ended. Henry, a Lancastrian, took Elizabeth of York as his wife and their marriage united the warring sides.

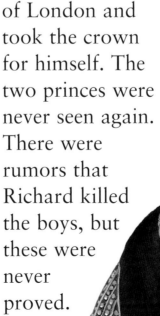

YOU MUST BE JOKING!

Lambert Simnel pretended he was Edward of Warwick, a Yorkist heir to the throne. He was even crowned and raised an army to fight Henry VII. Simnel lost, but Henry didn't kill him – he gave him a job in the royal kitchens instead!

A WICKED UNCLE?

Richard III was meant to help his nephew Edward V rule. Instead, he locked both his nephews in the Tower of London and took the crown for himself. The two princes were never seen again. There were rumors that Richard killed the boys, but these were never proved.

WHAT A HUSBAND

HENRY VIII MARRIED SIX times, more than any other English king. After 24 years of marriage, his first wife, Catherine of Aragon, had only produced a daughter. Keen for a son, Henry divorced her and married Anne Boleyn.

Anne, too, had a baby girl. Only Henry's third wife, Jane Seymour, produced the longed-for boy. Henry's last three wives didn't give him any children.

Henry split with the Roman Catholic Church for divorcing Catherine.

So he set up the Church of England, with himself at its head.

A courtly banquet
During his marriage to Catherine of Aragon, Henry VIII left running the country to his Lord Chancellor, Cardinal Thomas Wolsey. But in 1529 Wolsey fell from favor. Henry even seized Hampton Court, Wolsey's palace, for his own.

YOU MUST BE JOKING!
Henry's sixth wife, Catherine Parr, was more like a nurse than a queen. She dressed the bandages on the king's gross, ulcer-ridden leg.

THE MONASTERIES

After breaking away from Rome, Henry closed down England's abbeys and monasteries. Some were sold to bring in much-needed money. Others, such as Castle Acre Priory in Norfolk, were stripped of their treasures and then left to fall into disrepair.

CAN YOU BELIEVE IT?

Henry had one of his wives beheaded.

NO. Two of his wives had their heads chopped off – Anne Boleyn (his second wife) and Catherine Howard (his fifth wife).

YOU MUST BE JOKING!

Francis Drake, head of Elizabeth's navy, wasn't scared of the huge Spanish fleet sent to invade England in 1588. He coolly finished the game he was playing before he went off to defeat them!

Inspiring her men

When Elizabeth found out Philip of Spain planned to attack, she went to talk to her troops in person. She gave such a stirring speech that her men managed to repel the stronger Spanish fleet.

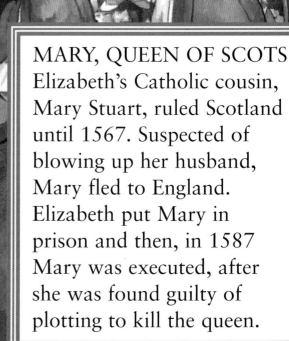

MARY, QUEEN OF SCOTS

Elizabeth's Catholic cousin, Mary Stuart, ruled Scotland until 1567. Suspected of blowing up her husband, Mary fled to England. Elizabeth put Mary in prison and then, in 1587 Mary was executed, after she was found guilty of plotting to kill the queen.

A**LL THREE OF HENRY VIII'S** children ruled England. Edward VI was nine when his father died. Sadly, he was a sickly boy, and died when he was just 15. Mary I took the throne next, but her reign was even shorter than Edward's.

Then Elizabeth I became queen in 1558. During her 45-year reign, England grew rich and powerful.

CAN YOU BELIEVE IT?
Sir Walter Raleigh named his colony in America after Elizabeth.

YES. He called it Virginia after her. Elizabeth was known as the "Virgin Queen," because she would not marry.

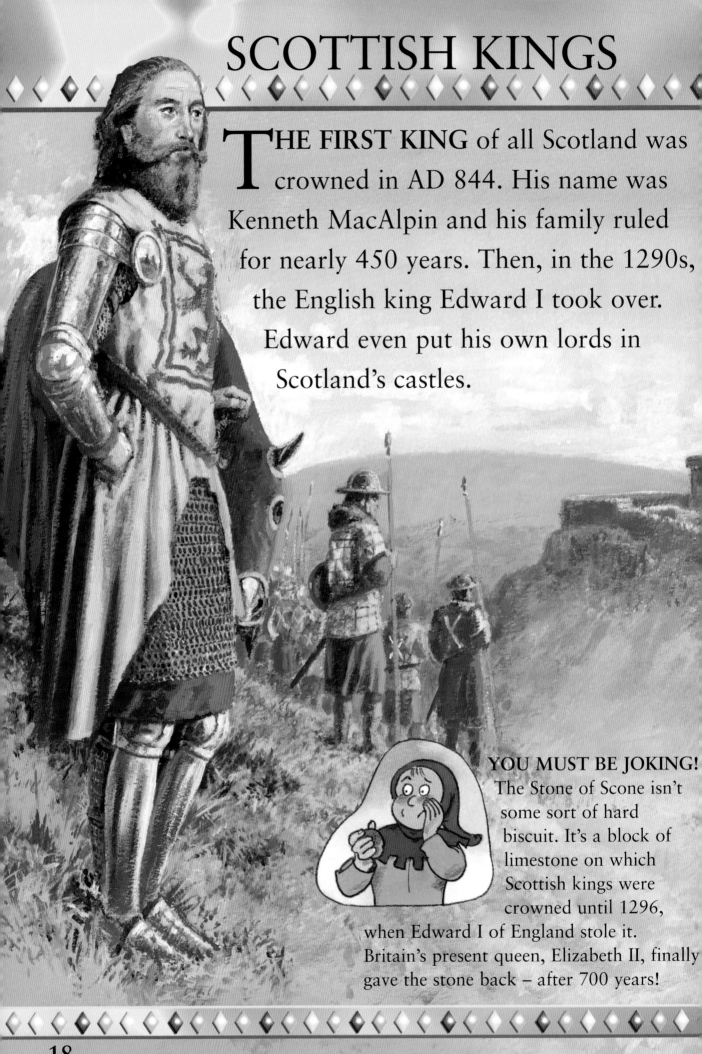

SCOTTISH KINGS

THE FIRST KING of all Scotland was crowned in AD 844. His name was Kenneth MacAlpin and his family ruled for nearly 450 years. Then, in the 1290s, the English king Edward I took over. Edward even put his own lords in Scotland's castles.

YOU MUST BE JOKING!
The Stone of Scone isn't some sort of hard biscuit. It's a block of limestone on which Scottish kings were crowned until 1296, when Edward I of England stole it. Britain's present queen, Elizabeth II, finally gave the stone back – after 700 years!

Two heroes, William Wallace and Robert Bruce, worked to drive out the English. England finally recognized Bruce as the Scottish king in 1328.

The siege of Stirling
In 1314 Robert Bruce laid siege to Stirling, a key castle in English hands. Then Bruce's army defeated the English at nearby Bannockburn.

THE REAL MACBETH
Shakespeare's play *Macbeth*, first performed in 1605, was based on a true story. Macbeth really did become king after killing his cousin, Duncan I. But Duncan died in battle, not in bed! Macbeth ruled from 1040 until 1057, when he was killed by Duncan's son, Malcolm III.

CAN YOU BELIEVE IT?
The Orkneys and Shetland Islands have always been part of Scotland.

NO. They were part of Norway. Scottish king James III was given the islands in 1469 when he married Princess Margaret of Norway. Some wedding present!

JAMES STUART

YOU MUST BE JOKING!
James was only one when he became king of Scotland! He was the son of Mary, Queen of Scots, and became king after his mom was forced from the country.

CAN YOU BELIEVE IT?
The Pilgrim Fathers were holy men who walked to Jerusalem.

NO. They were Puritans who did not like being ruled by James I. In 1620 they set sail for America and made a new life there instead.

The King James Bible
One of James I's greatest achievements was a new English translation of the Bible. Around 50 scholars worked on the book, which was published in 1611.

THE STUART FAMILY ruled Scotland from the 1370s. Then, in 1603, the Stuart king James VI became King James I of England, too. He inherited the English throne from his second-cousin, Elizabeth I.

James I wasn't everyone's favorite king. He didn't think he had to listen to Parliament – he preferred to take advice from flattering courtiers instead.

THE GUNPOWDER PLOT

In 1605 a group of 12 Catholics plotted to blow up James I. But the plot was discovered. Guy Fawkes, one of the conspirators, was caught red-handed with barrels of gunpowder beneath the Houses of Parliament. Each November 5, English people remember the failed Gunpowder Plot by burning stuffed "guys" on bonfires and setting off fireworks across the country.

CIVIL WAR

IN JANUARY 1649, Charles I became the only English king ever to have been put on trial and executed. This followed seven years of civil war, when the king's army had fought against the parliamentary army, led by Oliver Cromwell.

After Charles's execution, Cromwell was offered the job of king, but he refused. Until his death in 1658, he ruled under the title "Lord Protector."

Royalty returns
After Cromwell's death, his son tried to take over as Lord Protector, but he was useless. In 1660, Parliament asked Charles II to come back and rule as king.

YOU MUST BE JOKING!
Oliver Cromwell thought plays were a bad influence on people. During his rule, all the theaters were shut down.

CLOSED

CAN YOU BELIEVE IT?
Charles I wore an extra shirt when he walked to the scaffold.

YES. He said that he didn't want to shiver with cold in case anyone thought he was scared.

THE BATTLE OF NASEBY
The biggest battle of the Civil War happened at Naseby, in Northamptonshire, on June 14 1645.

In a day of tough tactics, Cromwell's New Model Army managed to defeat the King's men – and take two-thirds of the Royalist army prisoner!

BONNIE PRINCE CHARLIE
The Jacobites believed that descendants of James II should rule, instead of the Hanoverians. James II had ruled in the 1680s but was forced off the throne because he planned to make Britain Catholic. James's grandson, Bonnie Prince Charlie, tried to win back the throne, but he was defeated by George II's troops at the Battle of Culloden, in 1746.

BETWEEN 1714 and 1830, Britain was ruled by four kings called George. They are known as the Hanoverians, because George I had been born in Hanover, Germany. As James I's great-grandson, he became British king after the death of Queen Anne.

George III was probably the best-loved Hanoverian. He ruled wisely for 50 years, but then he went mad. The poor king spent the last 10 years of his reign locked away.

Buckingham Palace
George III bought Buckingham House in 1762 – but it didn't look like it does today. During the reign of George IV the architect John Nash turned the house into a palace fit for a king!

YOU MUST BE JOKING!
George III was known as "Farmer George." He earned the nickname because he was so interested in farming, and during his reign lots of new farming machinery was introduced.

CAN YOU BELIEVE IT?
George I spoke excellent English.

NO. He spoke his native German, and bothered to learn only a few English words and phrases.

ENGLISH PHRASE BOOK

QUEEN VICTORIA

Victoria and Disraeli
After Albert's death, Victoria relied on the advice of the Tory Prime Minister, Benjamin Disraeli. He was British PM twice – in 1868 and from 1874 to 1880. The queen trusted Disraeli and hated his rival, Gladstone.

VICTORIA BECAME QUEEN in 1837, when she was only 18 years old. At the time, Britain was the most powerful nation in the world and, during her long reign, it grew even greater. Victoria was not only a queen but an empress, ruler of a quarter of the whole world!

THE ROYAL ALBERT HALL
Prince Albert died of typhoid in 1861. The heartbroken queen wore black for the rest of her life and built many tributes to her husband. Best-known is London's circular Royal Albert Hall, overlooked by the lavish Albert Memorial.

In 1840, Victoria married Prince Albert. Their nine children married into just about every royal family in Europe. Victoria herself lived to such a ripe old age that her son Edward was a grandfather before he was a king!

YOU MUST BE JOKING!

There were lots of new inventions during Victoria's reign. She was the first British ruler to make a phone call, travel by train or ride in an elevator. She was also the first to be filmed and photographed!

CAN YOU BELIEVE IT?

Victoria and Albert lived in the Crystal Palace.

NO. The amazing glass building was built for the Great Exhibition of 1851, a show of all the latest machines and technology.

WORLD-WAR KINGS

DURING THE TWO WORLD WARS, kings George V and VI did all they could to keep people's spirits up.

In the First World War (1914–18), George V changed his German surname to Windsor and made 450 trips to see his fighting troops.

In the Second World War (1939–45), George VI and his queen stayed in London – even after the palace was bombed.

During the Blitz Every day, George VI and his queen, Elizabeth, walked through London, helping people whose homes had been destroyed by enemy bombing.

KING FOR A YEAR
Edward VIII reigned for 325 days, then gave up the throne to marry Wallis Simpson. He couldn't marry Wallis and be king because she was American and because she'd been divorced – twice. So poor Edward's brother had to be king instead.

YOU MUST BE JOKING!
George V gave the first Christmas broadcast. He spoke to the people on the radio. His grand-daughter, Elizabeth II, was the first to make a Christmas broadcast on TV.

CAN YOU BELIEVE IT?
The Irish Republic was born in George V's reign.

YES. In 1921 Ireland was split to try to sort out the problems there. Southern Ireland became an independent republic, and Northern Ireland stayed under British rule.

CAN YOU BELIEVE IT?
Prince Philip's surname wasn't Mountbatten.

YES. He took the name of his uncle, Dickie Mountbatten. It was less of a mouthful than his original surname, Schleswig-Holstein-Sonderburg-Glücksburg!

QUEEN ELIZABETH II was crowned in Westminster Abbey in 1953. During her reign, the job of ruling has changed. Parts of the world that once belonged to Britain's empire are now independent countries.

The Queen's main job is to represent Britain around the world. She visits different countries with her husband, Prince Philip. She will be succeeded by her eldest son, Charles, or by his elder son, William.

THE CROWN JEWELS

Most of the time, the Crown Jewels are on show in the Tower of London but the Queen uses them on special occasions. They include the Royal Scepter that Elizabeth held at her coronation. At its end is a giant, heart-shaped diamond – one of the biggest in the world!

Opening Parliament

One of the Queen's duties is to open Parliament. The Queen doesn't run the country, but the Prime Minister visits her each week and lets her know all that's going on.

YOU MUST BE JOKING!

The Queen's a trained car mechanic! She helped out at the end of the Second World War by serving in the forces and taking a course in vehicle maintenance.

INDEX

Alfred the Great 6–7
Anglo-Saxons 5, 6–7
Arthur 5

Boleyn, Anne 14, 15
Bosworth 12
Bruce, Robert 18–19

Canute 7
Catherine of Aragon 14
Charles I 22, 23
Charles II 22–23
Charlie, Bonnie Prince 24
Civil War 22, 23
Cromwell, Oliver 22, 23
Crown Jewels 31
Crusades 10, 11
Crystal Palace 27

Disraeli, Benjamin 26–27
Drake, Francis 16

Edward I 18
Edward V 13
Edward VI 17
Edward VIII 28
Edward the Confessor 8

Egbert 6
Elizabeth I 16–17, 21
Elizabeth II 18, 29, 30–31

George I 24, 25
George II 24
George III 24–25
George IV 25
George V 28, 29
George VI 28–29
Great Exhibition 27
Gunpowder Plot 21

Hampton Court 14
Harold II 8, 9
Henry VII 12, 13
Henry VIII 14–15
Hood, Robin 11
Howard, Catherine 15

James I 20–21
James II 24
John 10–11

MacAlpin, Kenneth 18
Macbeth 19
Magna Carta 10–11
Malcolm III 19
Mary I 17
Mary, Queen of Scots 16, 20

Offa's Dyke 6

Parliament 21, 22, 30–31
Parr, Catherine 14
Philip, Prince 30, 31
Pilgrim Fathers 20

Raleigh, Walter 17
Richard I 10, 11
Richard III 12, 13
Romans 4, 5

Seymour, Jane 14
Simnel, Lambert 13
Simpson, Wallis 28
Spanish Armada 16–17

Tower of London 8–9, 13, 31

Victoria 26–27
Vikings 6, 7, 9

Wallace, William 19
Wars of the Roses 12–13
William the Conqueror 8–9
Wolsey, Thomas 14–15